CHERYL BRISCO'S BOOK *of* CONFIDENCE

Cheryl Brisco

authorHOUSE®

AuthorHouse™ LLC
1663 Liberty Drive
Bloomington, IN 47403
www.authorhouse.com
Phone: 1-800-839-8640

Published by AuthorHouse   08/20/2014

ISBN: 978-1-4969-3302-7 (sc)
ISBN: 978-1-4969-3301-0 (e)

FOREWORDS

This Book is about Confidence, something that alot of people don't have in there lives today. I am writing this book to help inspire, those people out there that don't have any confidence at all in there live's.God did not put you here to not believe in him. first of all and second of all not to believe in yourself, and your ability to create the life that you want so badly. All you need to do is just (BELIEVE), its a powerful thing that will shape and change your life.most people don't have no happiness in there lives at all because they want just believe in themselves. You can do anything that you set your mind, Heart and faith in.dont let other people talk you out of your confidence, because its your back bone in this life.

Confidence is being
sure of yourself; no
matter what happens
to you in your life.

1

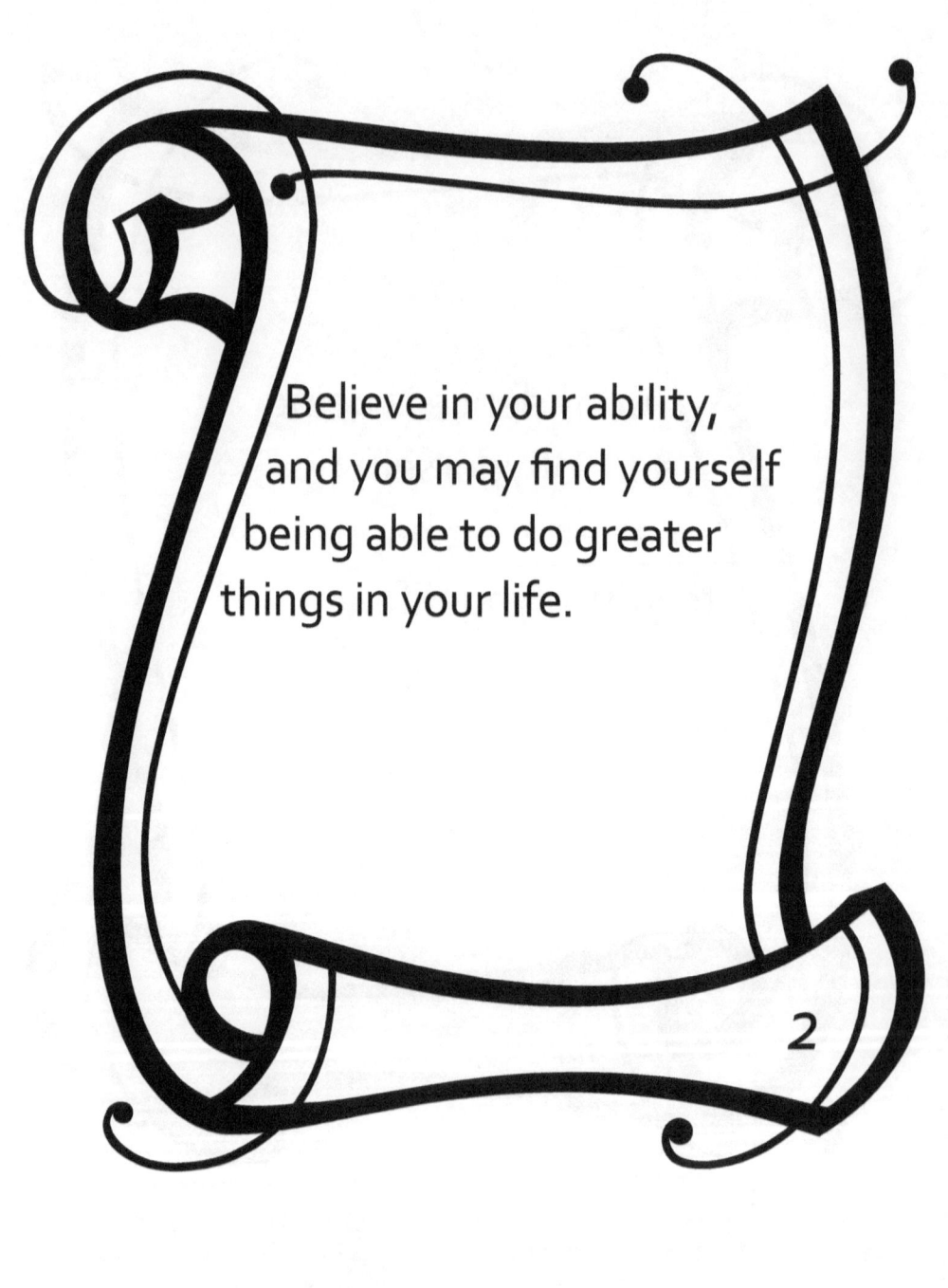

Believe in your ability, and you may find yourself being able to do greater things in your life.

2

If you believe you will fail, you will be feeding yourself a self profilling prophecy.

3

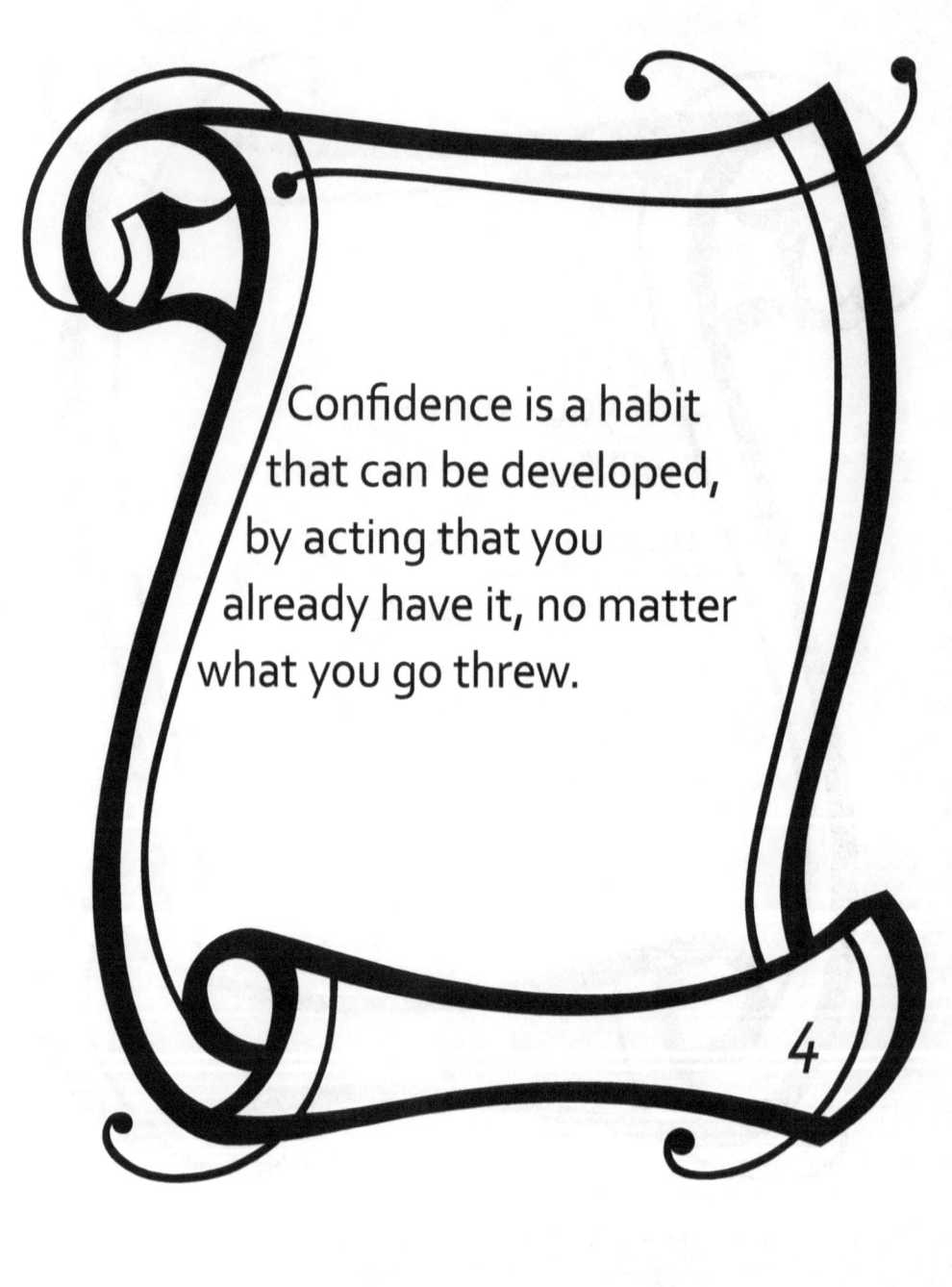

Confidence is a habit
that can be developed,
by acting that you
already have it, no matter
what you go threw.

4

A truly confident
person is not unduly
upset by setbacks.

5

A Confident person
listen to criticism, but
don't let it stop them.

6

Love all, trust in God. Do wrong to no one. And be confident at all times.

7

A small ounce of
confidence is worth
a million dollars.

8

Get your confidence
up and you will get
your Money up.

9

Self-Confidence is the key
to Love, Joy, Happiness,
& great success.

10

Donot be afraid of
any situation going on
in your life, and in all
means dont let fear scare
your confidence off.

11

Confidence is being prepared for any circumstances. Because circumstances are almost out of your control.

As a member of the
human race, you are
equal to all others,
so stay encouraged &
highly confident.

13

Self confidence is believing
in yourself when no one
else will believe in you.

14

Confidence is that
small, quiet voice in
you that tells you all the
time you can do it.

15

Being patience is a huge
sign of strong confidence.

16

Confidence is
knowing that things
will go your way.

17

You can measure a
person's confidence by
what it takes to discourage
them. So show them
your strong confidence.

18

Some of us are born confident. But most of us learn how to be confident.

19

Confidence is like a
wheel on a car it spins,
no matter what.

20

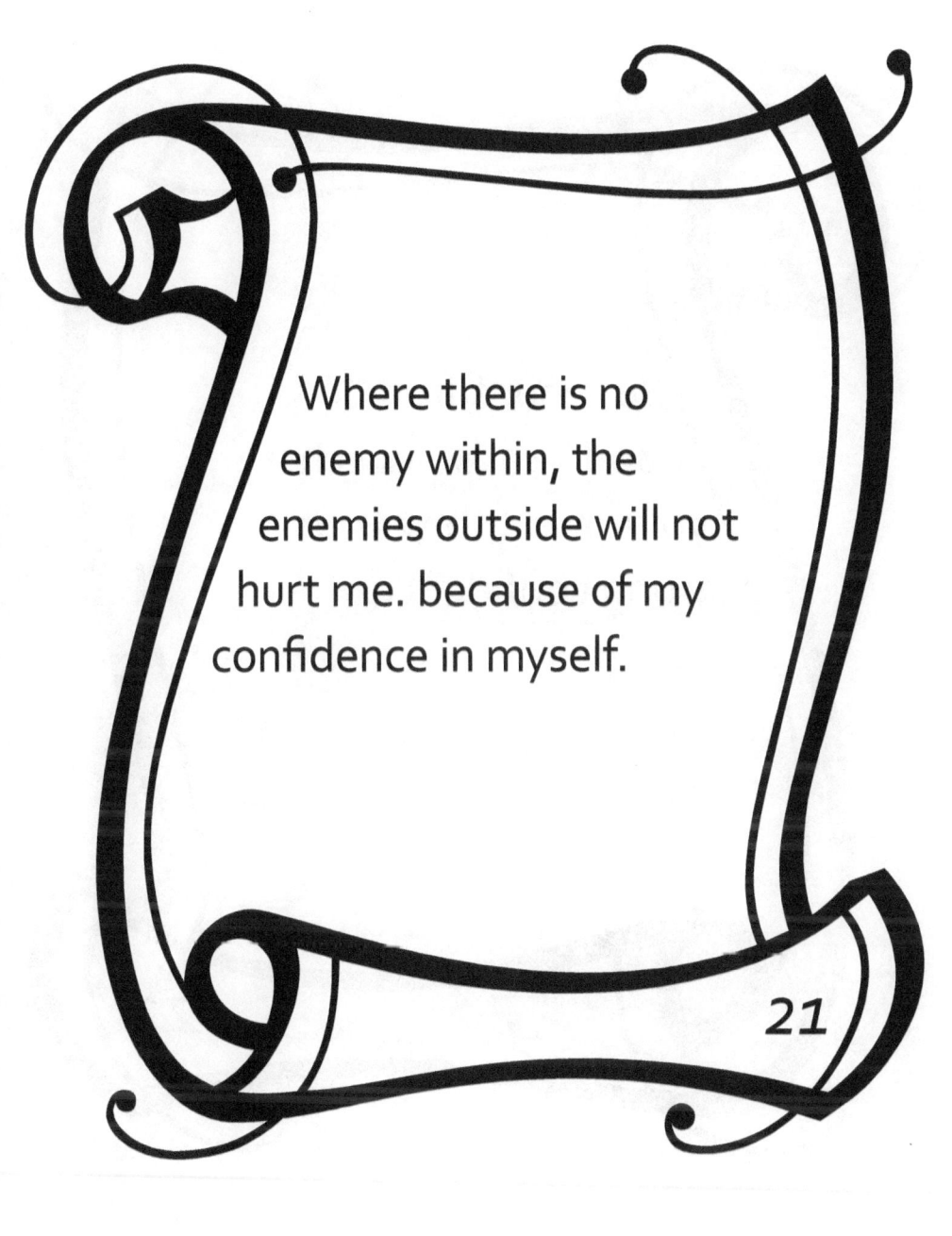

Where there is no
enemy within, the
enemies outside will not
hurt me. because of my
confidence in myself.

21

Put your future in
good hands - which is
your own threw your
strong confidence.

22

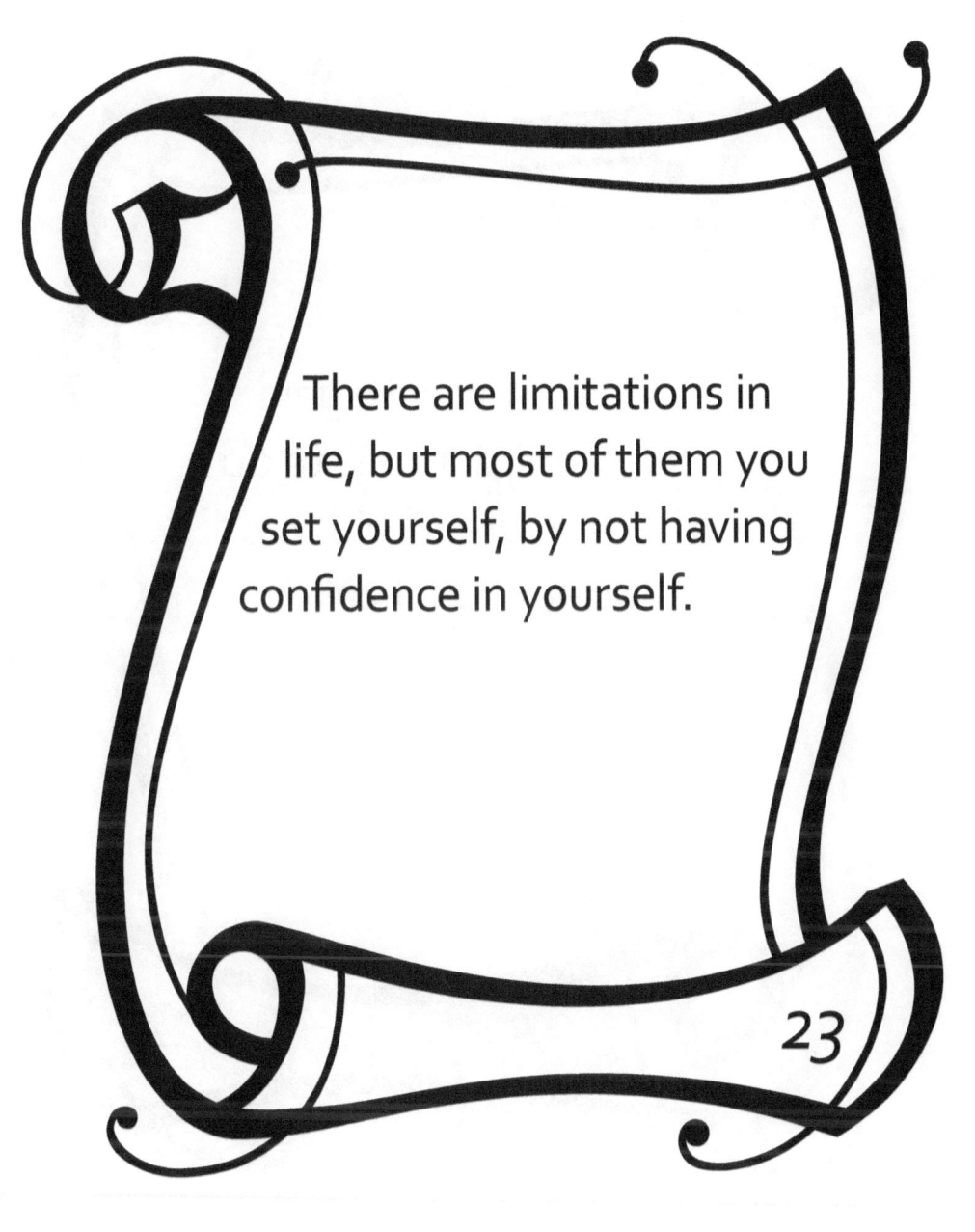

There are limitations in life, but most of them you set yourself, by not having confidence in yourself.

23

The best way to gain self- confidence is to do what you are afraid to do no matter what it takes.

24

Your greatest confidence
will come when you
show yourself that you
love yourself daily.

25

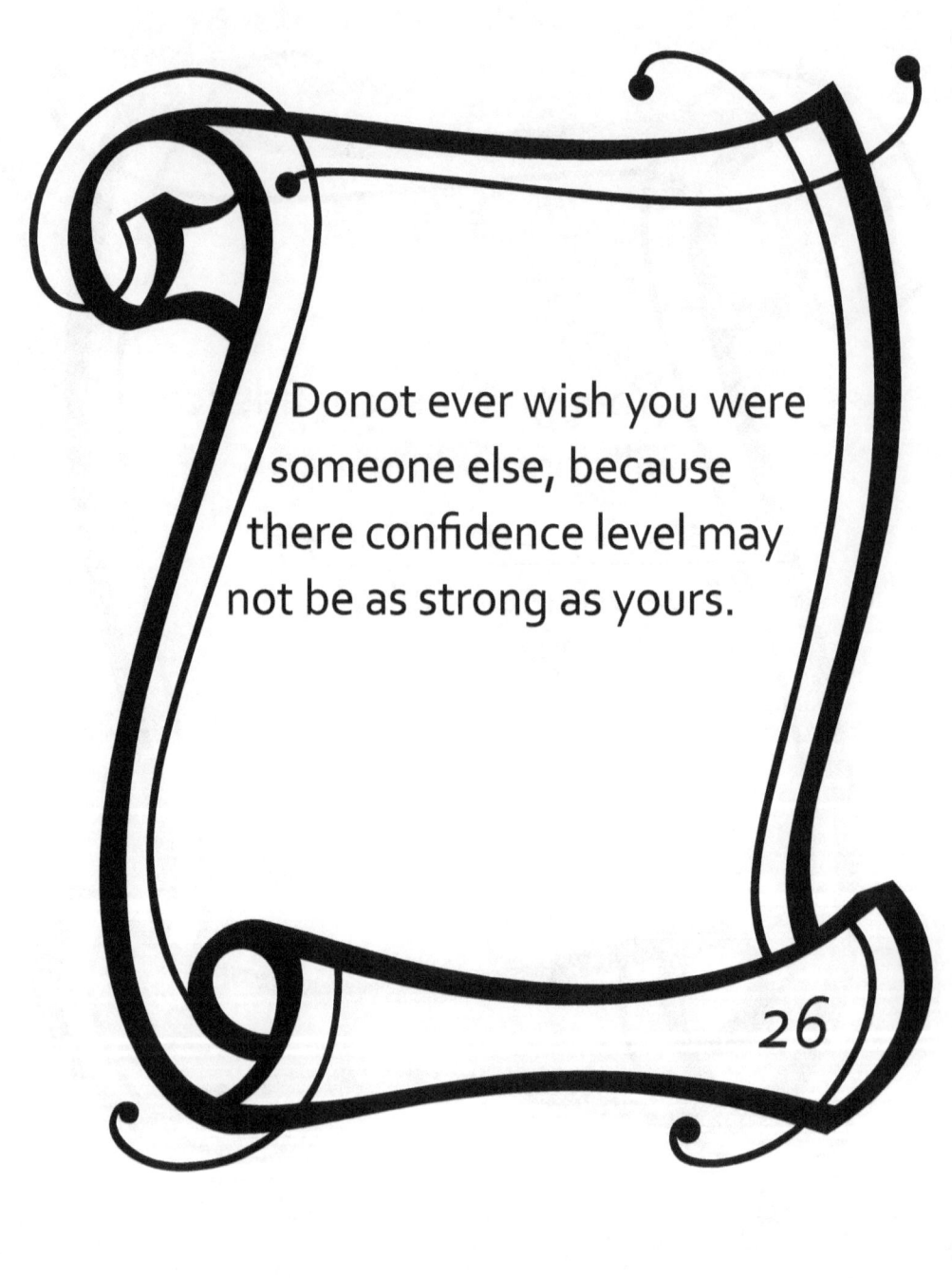

Donot ever wish you were someone else, because there confidence level may not be as strong as yours.

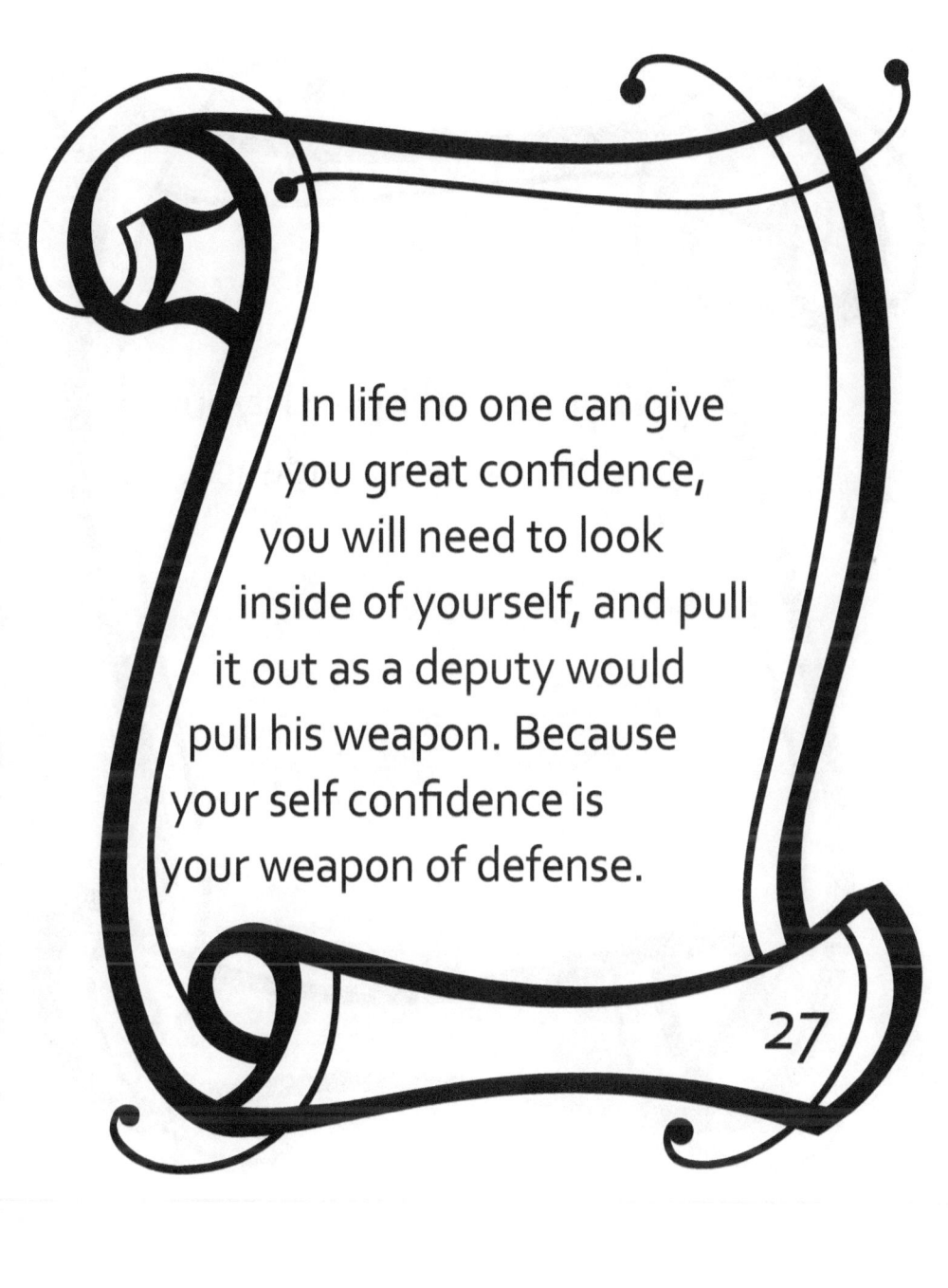

In life no one can give
you great confidence,
you will need to look
inside of yourself, and pull
it out as a deputy would
pull his weapon. Because
your self confidence is
your weapon of defense.

27

All you need in life is your
God and your confidence.

28

Dont let fear of others
steal, or kill your
confidence in yourself.
Keep on pushing forward.

29

A great deal of talent is lost to the world for lack of confidence in themselves.

30

A great deal of talent
is lost to the world for
want of a little courage
& (CONFIDENCE)

31

The secret of success
is to believe in God
and then yourself.
After that everything
else is Confidence.

32

Be bold be modest,
but don't hold a low
opinion of yourself. Just
stay in confidence.

33

Confront your fears. It is the only way to achieve your strongest confidence.

34

You dont need a degree
in psychology to bring
up all your confidence.

35

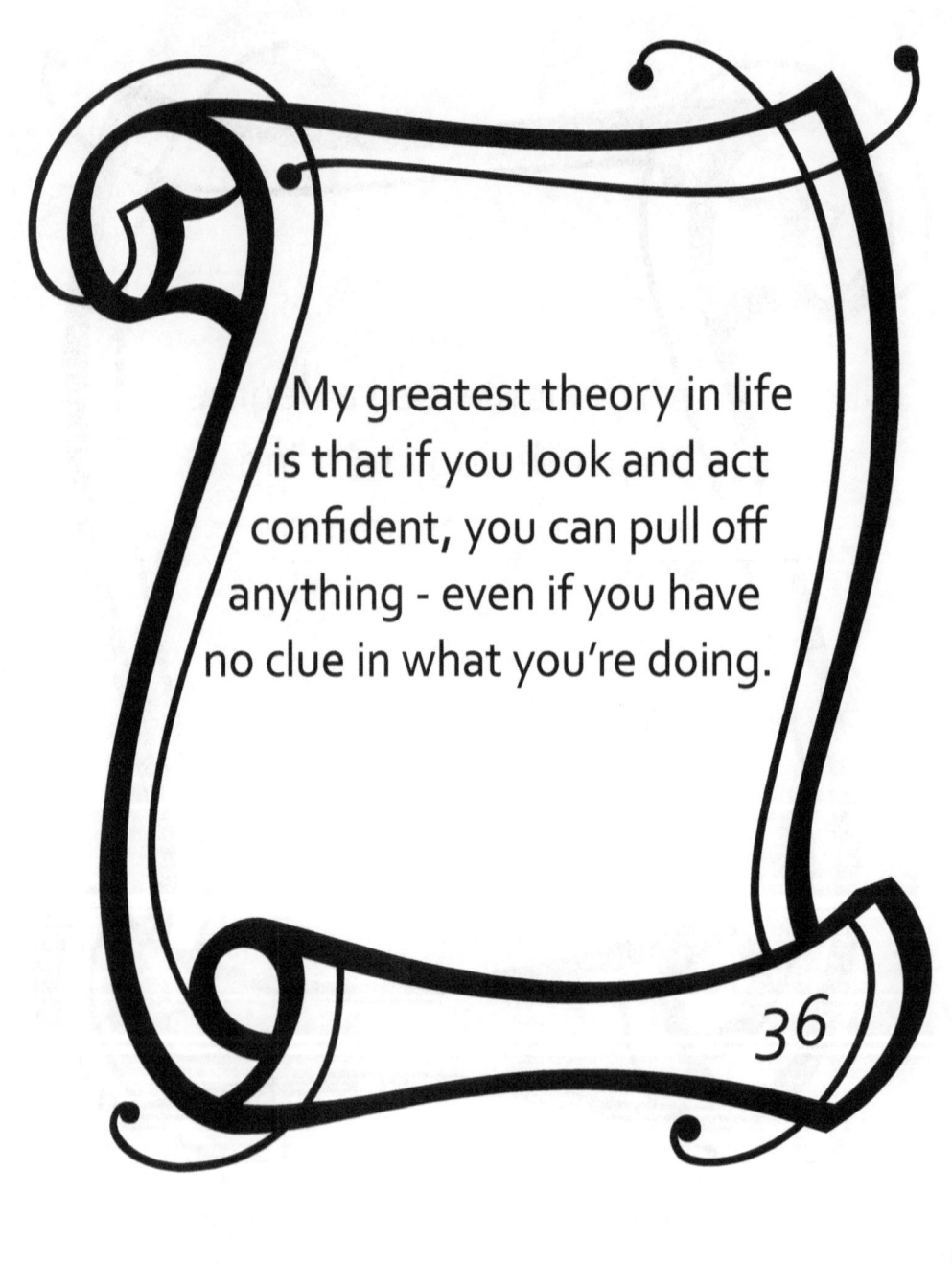

My greatest theory in life
is that if you look and act
confident, you can pull off
anything - even if you have
no clue in what you're doing.

36

Even if you don't feel confident, just try to look as though you do anyway.

37

Self- Confidence is the master key to undertaking great things in life.

38

Confidence is what you
need to have before you
understand the situation
and the problem.

39

A wise man or woman
makes his or her
own decisions, threw
strong confidence.

40

It's not what you think
you are that holds you
back. Its alway's where
your confidence level is.

41

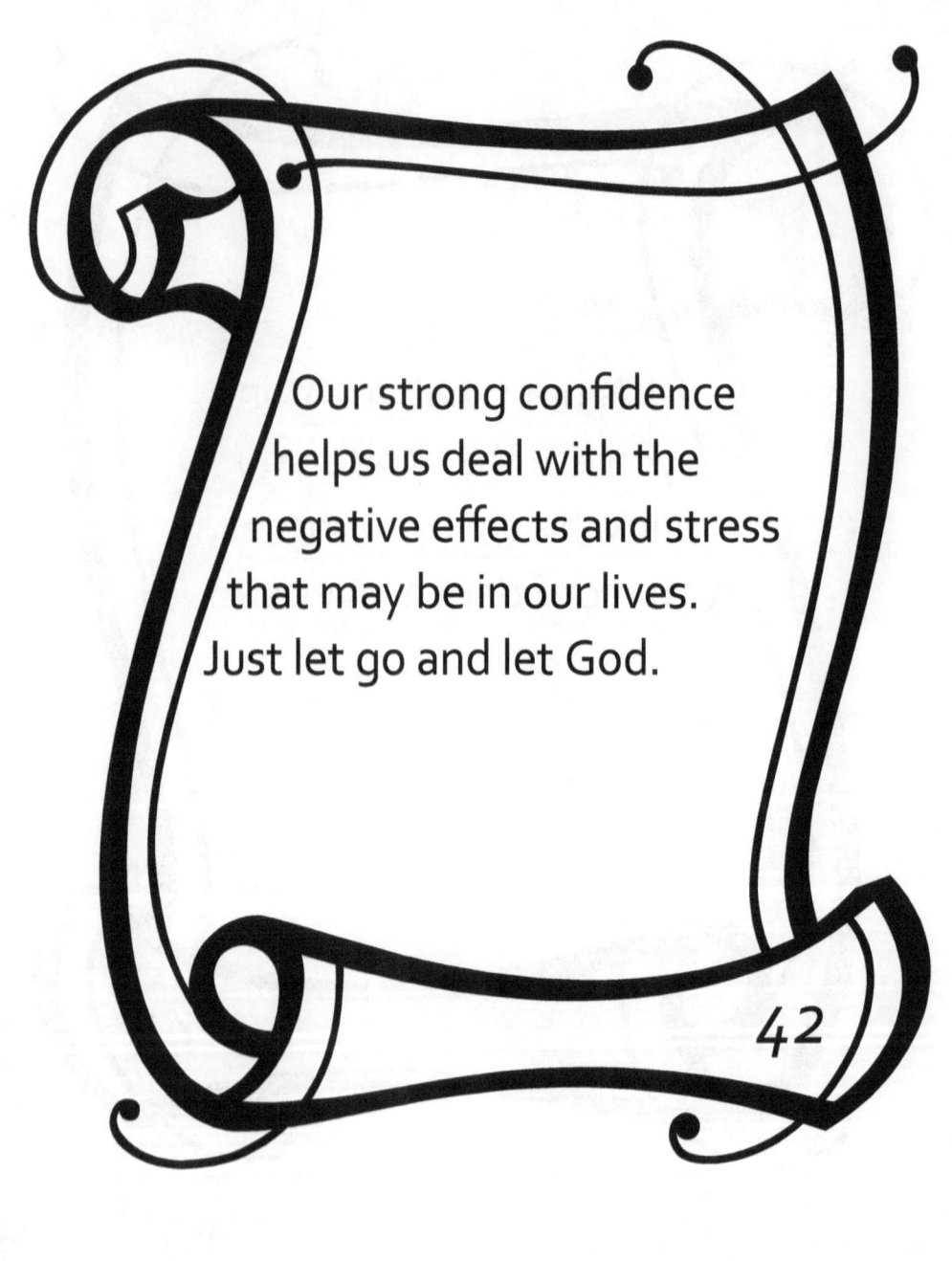

Our strong confidence
helps us deal with the
negative effects and stress
that may be in our lives.
Just let go and let God.

42

Most of us, as we
get older we should
gain more confidence
about ourselves.

43

A bird and there feathers
flock together, so shall
man & woman flock
to there confidence.

44

No human being, on this
earth can be confident
of themselves, until
they give themselves
permission to be confident.

45

Confidence is the door bell, in front of your house so just ring it.

46

Everyone may feel
insecure at times but
don't let your confidence
guard down.

47

With self-confidence you have already won in life. So go win again, over and over again, (you get the picture.)

48

With confidence you
can paint a perfect
picture of how you
want your life to be.

49

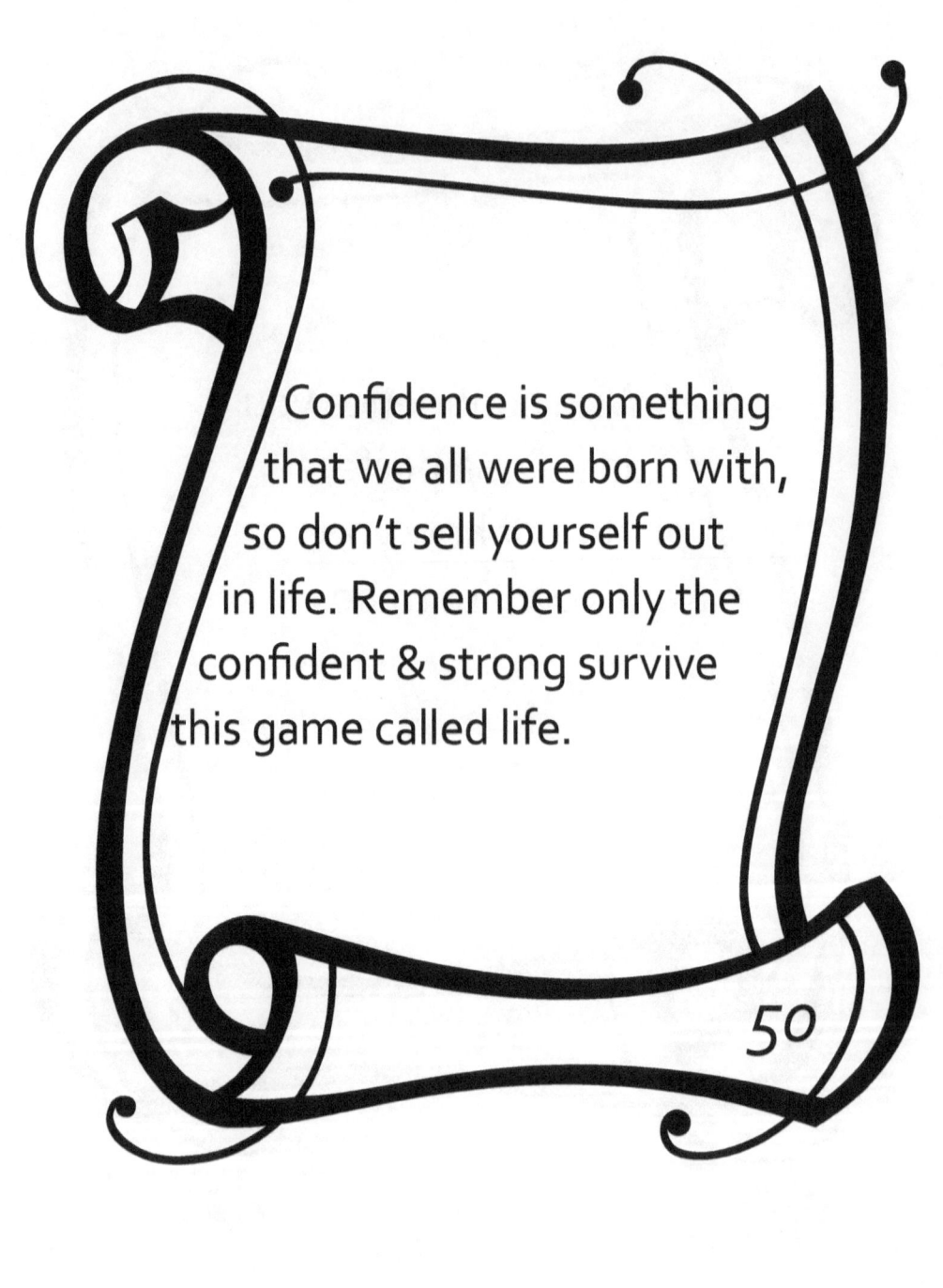

Confidence is something that we all were born with, so don't sell yourself out in life. Remember only the confident & strong survive this game called life.

50